Sterling North

and the Story of Rascal

Other Badger Biographies

Sterling North

and the Story of Rascal

SHEILA TERMAN COHEN

Wisconsin Historical Society Press

Published by the Wisconsin Historical Society Press
Publishers since 1855

wisconsin**history**.org

Photographs identified with WHi or WHS are from the Society's collections; address requests to reproduce these photos to the Visual Materials Archivist at the Wisconsin Historical Society, 816 State Street, Madison, WI 53706.

Back cover photo: Courtesy of the North Archives; photograph by Clarence E. Olson
Printed in the United States of America
Design and layout by Jill Bremigan

19 18 17 16 15   1 2 3 4 5

Library of Congress Cataloging-in-Publication Data

Cohen, Sheila, 1939–
    Sterling North and the story of Rascal / Sheila Terman Cohen.
        pages cm. — (Badger biographical series)
    Includes index.
    ISBN 978-0-87020-735-8 (pbk. : alk. paper)—ISBN 978-0-87020-736-5 (ebook) 1. North, Sterling, 1906-1974—Juvenile literature. 2. Authors, American—20th century—Biography—Juvenile literature. 3. Rascal (Raccoon) I. Title.
    PS3527.O585Z57 2015
    813'.52—dc23
    [B]
                                    2015013779

To Sterling North's daughter, Arielle Olson,
and Edgerton resident Walter Diedrick,
who have each helped to keep
Sterling North's memory alive.

Contents

1

Sterling North and His Four-Legged Pal

When Sterling North was 11 years old, he had no idea that his adventures with a most unusual pet would someday make him famous.

Sterling grew up in the small town of Edgerton, Wisconsin, in the early 1900s. Many kids in Edgerton had pet dogs or cats. Some had pet goldfish or birds like canaries. But Sterling's pet was different.

Sterling's pet did not come from a pet store. His name was Rascal, and he was a furry, ring-tailed raccoon. Sterling plucked Rascal from a burrow in the ground after

Sterling North at 10 years old

Rascal's mother and her 3 other **kits abandoned** their den. Sterling knew Rascal would never survive without food or water. So he brought the frightened little creature home.

This began Sterling's year-long adventure with his beloved 4-legged friend.

This copy of *Rascal: A Memoir of a Better Era* is on display at the Sterling North Museum in Edgerton.

When Sterling grew up, he became a famous writer who worked in New York City. But he never forgot the time that he and Rascal spent together. When Sterling was 56 years old, he decided to write about his childhood memories and his adventures with his favorite pet raccoon.

There is a good chance you or someone in your family has read

kit (kit): a young, fur-bearing animal   **abandoned** (uh **ban** duhnd): left and never returned to

2

Sterling's book, *Rascal:A Memoir of a Better Era.* It was published in 1963. The book became so popular that Walt Disney Productions made it into a movie.

Before long, Sterling's lovable pet Rascal won his way into the hearts of people young and old all over the world.

2

The North Family Tree

Sterling North's mother, Elizabeth Nelson, was born in 1866. Elizabeth's nickname was Libby. She loved language and nature, and she was very smart. Libby wanted to learn more about both of her passions. In 1880 she enrolled at Lawrence College in Appleton, Wisconsin, at the young age of 14. Four years later, Libby graduated first in her class with degrees in **linguistics** and **biology**.

COURTESY OF THE NORTH ARCHIVES

Sterling's mother, Libby, was one of his greatest influences.

At Lawrence College, Libby met another student named David Willard North. After graduation, both Libby and David enrolled at the University of Wisconsin in Madison as **post-graduate** students.

linguistics (ling **gwis** tiks): the study of human speech and languages **biology** (bı **ah** luh jee): a science that deals with things that are alive, such as plants and animals **post-graduate** (pohst **gra** juh wuht): continuing formal education after graduating from college

Lawrence College, ca. 1860

In the 1800s, many women did not go to college. But Libby was eager for more education. She got a master's degree in biology, while David studied **pharmacy**.

David grew up on a farm close to Edgerton, Wisconsin, near the shore of Lake **Koshkonong**. His grandfather, Thomas North Sr., was one of the early settlers in Wisconsin. Thomas Sr. arrived from Sheffield, England, in the 1840s with his 18-year-old son, Thomas Jr., who would later become David's father.

pharmacy (**fahr** muh see): the science of preparing and providing medicine   **Koshkonong**: **kahsh** kuh nawng

5

COURTESY OF THE NORTH ARCHIVES

Sterling's father, David Willard North, in a photograph taken when he was an older man

Together, Thomas Sr. and his son walked more than 80 miles from Milwaukee to the **wilderness** near Lake Koshkonong in southern Wisconsin. There they staked out a 380-acre plot and built the family's sturdy log cabin. Later, they built a larger house on the property, too. This house became home to 3 **generations** of Norths, including young David and his parents. Each generation farmed the soil, hunted animals for food, and searched the land for **arrowheads** that were left by the American Indians who lived there when settlers came to the region.

As a boy, David was intrigued by the arrowheads and other symbols of tribal life that surrounded him on the farm. This boyhood interest turned into an adult passion. When he grew

wilderness: wil dur nuhs   **generations:** je nuh **ray** shuhnz   **arrowhead:** **er** oh hed

up, David became an expert on Indian mounds and trails. His collection of arrowheads was one of the best in the area. And his knowledge of Indian **lore** was respected throughout the region.

An arrowhead like the ones David collected

David also had a strong **curiosity** about nature. When David was a young boy, a famous **naturalist** and **ornithologist** from Sweden moved into the farm next door. The man's name was **Theodore Thure Kumlien**. He taught David about every bird that crossed their land.

When Libby and David met, they learned they had many interests in common. Above all, they shared a love for the natural world. They were married on July 15, 1887, and moved to a small farm in Albion, Wisconsin. Soon they would delight in sharing their interests and knowledge with their children.

lore (lor): common traditions or beliefs   curiosity (kyur ee **ah** suh tee): an eager desire to learn   **naturalist** (**na** chuh ruh list): a person who studies plants and animals as they live in nature   ornithologist (or nuh **thah** luh jist): a person who studies birds   **Theodore Thure Kumlien**: thee uh dor too **rah koom** lın

3
Giving Words to Nature's Wonders

Thomas Sterling North was born on November 4, 1906. The day began as a typical autumn day in southern Wisconsin. Most of the big, old trees on Libby and David's farm had already lost their leaves. The nearby shore of Lake Koshkonong had turned from an inviting summer blue to a deep gray. Soon, snow and ice would cover the land and water.

David was often away from home, trying to stir up one business idea or another in Edgerton and elsewhere. The day of Sterling's birth was no different. David arrived home in the family's horse-drawn buggy just after Sterling was born.

The family farmhouse was drafty. It gave little protection from the cold air that **seeped** into its small rooms. Moments after Sterling was born, he was dipped into a bath of warm unsalted lard. This was a common practice in those days

seeped: flowed slowly through a small opening

to keep the newborn baby warm.

Sterling, who was called by his middle name, thrived during his first 3 years living on the

Sterling spent his earliest years in this farmhouse.

farm. Libby introduced him to the natural world and to the literature that she loved. Later Sterling wrote that he learned to appreciate both nature and the written word during his first 3 years of life.

Sterling had 3 older siblings: 2 sisters, Jessica and Theo, and a brother, Herschel. They were already in high school when Sterling was born. When Sterling was young, his siblings left for college. This gave Libby plenty of time to spend with Sterling as she did chores around the house and farm.

Every season held the adventure of new things to be learned. In the spring, Sterling would sit at his mother's feet and watch her tend to the **anemones** and fragrant white **hyacinths** that bloomed in the garden. Libby would point to the **stamen** and **pistil** inside the fragile petals of each flower. These would help create more blossoms, she explained to him.

COURTESY OF THE NORTH ARCHIVES

Sisters Theo and Jessica and brother Herschel, before Sterling was born

anemone (uh **nem** uh nee): a plant that blooms in spring and has large white or colored flowers
hyacinth (**hı** uh sinth): a plant with stalks of fragrant flowers shaped like bells   **stamen** (**stay** muhn): the part of a flower that produces pollen   **pistil** (**pis** tuhl): the part in the center of a flower that produces the seed

On warm summer nights, Sterling would listen to the loud chorus of crickets and frogs. Outside, he learned to recognize each constellation in the northern **hemisphere**. The dark sky of rural Wisconsin made a wonderful backdrop for seeing constellations such as Ursa Major (the Big Bear), Ursa Minor (the Little Bear), and Cassiopeia (the queen whose throne is shaped like a W).

Hyacinths

In the winter, when the fields were covered in white snow, Libby showed Sterling that each snowflake had 6 points, and that no 2 flakes were exactly alike.

Later, Sterling summed up what he learned from his mother. "Every bird, beast, flower and tree has its very own reason for existing, and so does every single human being."

Libby's appreciation for nature would remain with Sterling for the rest of his life

hemisphere (**he** muh sfir): one of the halves of the sky, imagined as a giant dome, that can be seen from earth

4

An Accident Waiting to Happen

Pets were always present at the North farmhouse. But one pet in particular stood out in Sterling's earliest memories. Curly was a mixed-breed dog with deep brown eyes. She was named for her thick coat of black curls. Her job was to round up the cows in the pasture when it was time for milking.

WHI IMAGE ID 91514

Sterling's dog Curly probably looked a lot like this dog.

Sterling later wrote that the big black dog helped him take his first steps. "One of my first memories was that of grasping the glistening pelt of my constant friend and childhood companion Curly."

Sterling loved Curly, but the rest of the family was often **baffled** by the dog's unusual behavior. After all, how

baffled (**ba** fuhld): completely confused

many farm dogs would clamp their jaws onto the tail of a cow for a free ride back to the barn? And what kind of self-respecting creature would steal eggs from the hen house for a treat?

Life on a dairy farm was always busy. When the grown-ups were working, sometimes Curly was Sterling's only companion. That's when the curious young Sterling would explore his surroundings, straying off to places where no 2-year-old boy belonged.

One day, Sterling wanted to see the stock tank, where the horses and cows refreshed themselves with drinks of cold water. Sometimes freshly caught fish were kept in the stock tank until they could be cleaned for dinner.

COURTESY OF THE NORTH ARCHIVES

A curly-headed and mischievous Sterling at 2 years old

Sterling was too small to reach the top of the tank, but he wanted to see the fish inside. He dragged a wooden box to the side of the tank. Then he climbed on top of the box and looked over the edge and into the water. He saw the fish, and he was fascinated! So he bent down to get a better look.

Suddenly, Sterling lost his balance and tumbled headfirst into the ice-cold water. When Curly saw what had happened, she jumped up, tugged at Sterling's pants, and dragged the crying boy to safety.

Some little boys might have stayed in the yard close to the house after a dangerous adventure like that. But not Sterling!

The adults told him many times never to go into the pasture where the family bull lived. But Sterling was too young to realize the risks of getting in the way of such a dangerous animal. One day he crawled under the wooden fence and ventured into the pasture. The bull looked at Sterling with mounting **irritation**. As Sterling crept closer and closer, the massive beast began to paw the soil angrily. Then, with his eyes focused right on Sterling, the bull slowly bent

irritation (ir uh **tay** shuhn): anger or annoyance

his large head toward the ground. The bull pointed his horns straight ahead. He was ready to charge!

Once again, Curly was there. The dog barked loudly at the angry bull. When that didn't work, Curly did what she had done so often when herding the cows. She clamped her teeth on the end of the bull's tail. This caused the huge animal to clomp around in circles, trying to release Curly's

A bull, similar to the animal that charged Sterling

firm grip. While Curly distracted the bull, Sterling was able to run to safety as fast as his short legs could carry him.

Believe it or not, that was not the last time Sterling's curiosity got the best of him. The dirt road that ran in front of the farmhouse had always been an attraction for him, but his parents always told him to stay away from it. The road was used by farmers in large horse-drawn carts to take their eggs, corn, and other goods to Edgerton.

When he was 3 years old, Sterling felt the **temptation** to investigate the road and what lay beyond the North's small farmyard. One day Sterling and Curly set out down the road to a place called Short Run's Creek, not far away.

On the way back they heard the frantic cry of a farmer coming up behind them. "Runaway horses!" the farmer cried out. Suddenly, the farmer's team of **Clydesdale** horses came **barreling** down the dirt road toward Sterling and Curly. Dust flew everywhere! Sterling froze with fear, unable to move out of the road.

Once again, Curly saved the day. She grabbed the seat of Sterling's blue denim overalls. Then she pulled the frightened little boy to the arms of his frantic

A Clydesdale horse

temptation (tem **tay** shuhn): strong desire   **Clydesdale: klidz** dayl   **barreling**: moving at a high speed

mother, who had come running when she heard the horses' **commotion**.

After that, the North family looked away whenever Curly helped herself to eggs or grabbed onto a cow's tail. She had earned her place as a beloved hero, free from punishment for the rest of her life.

There were only a few times when Curly wasn't around to prevent an accident. One of those accidents happened in the North kitchen when Sterling was very small. He was in his high chair when he spotted an interesting porcelain doorknob not far from where he sat. Entranced by the shining object, Sterling leaned over to grab it. All of a sudden he and the high chair went tumbling over, crushing Sterling's pudgy finger between the chair's frame and the wooden kitchen floor.

For the rest of Sterling's life, the shorter fourth finger on his right hand would be a reminder of his early adventurous spirit—a spirit that, like his short finger, would forever remain a part of who he was.

commotion (kuh **moh** shuhn): noisy excitement and confusion

5

No More Hyacinths

Although Sterling's father David had studied pharmacy, the regular work hours of a pharmacist did not appeal to someone with David's free-roaming spirit. David, or D.W., as the town folks called him, had other dreams. When Sterling was 3 years old, David moved the family from the farm in Albion to Edgerton 3 miles down the road, eventually settling in a house on Rollin Street.

WHI IMAGE ID 30854

Birdseye View, Edgerton, Wis.

A postcard shows a bird's-eye view of Edgerton.

Edgerton was a small town of less than 1,000 people. There, David tried his hand at many things, always with great enthusiasm. For example, he even served as Edgerton's **justice of the peace**.

David's charm and good looks made it easy for him to buy and sell almost anything. He invested money in a New York bakery that was the first to package fresh bread for grocery stores. He purchased many acres of wheat fields in Montana. He bought real estate properties with loans from the bank that he often couldn't pay back.

David's many business efforts could make life difficult for his family. He was often away from home for long periods of time. This meant Libby stayed behind to take care of their family and their home. Sometimes David's businesses succeeded, and sometimes they failed. It meant Sterling sometimes wondered if they would have enough money to buy an appealing piece of candy or new pair of winter mittens.

Young Sterling didn't know it, but life was about to become even more challenging.

justice of the peace: someone who is elected or appointed to perform marriages and make decisions on minor court cases

When Sterling wasn't being **mischievous** or exploring outside, he would often listen as his mother Libby read to him. The comfort and enjoyment he felt from hearing the words on the pages possibly paved the way for Sterling's future career as a writer.

Sterling began reading for himself at a very early age. He memorized 10 verses of the poem *Marmion* by the age of 4. Eventually, Sterling began to make up his own rhymes. In 1914, Libby submitted one of Sterling's poems, *A Song of Summer*, to the *St. Nicholas* magazine for young readers when Sterling was just 7 years old. Unfortunately, she would not live to see her son's first published poem appear several months later.

In the early spring of that year, Libby North was struck with **pneumonia**. At that time there was no medicine to cure the disease. Sadly, Libby died on the last day of March in 1914.

mischievous (mis chuh vuhs): showing a spirit of fun or playfulness   pneumonia (nu moh nyuh): a serious illness affecting the lungs that is marked by fever, cough, and difficulty in breathing

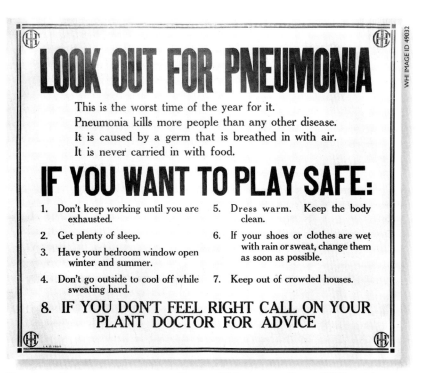

LOOK OUT FOR PNEUMONIA

This is the worst time of the year for it.
Pneumonia kills more people than any other disease.
It is caused by a germ that is breathed in with air.
It is never carried in with food.

IF YOU WANT TO PLAY SAFE:

1. Don't keep working until you are exhausted.
2. Get plenty of sleep.
3. Have your bedroom window open winter and summer.
4. Don't go outside to cool off while sweating hard.
5. Dress warm. Keep the body clean.
6. If your shoes or clothes are wet with rain or sweat, change them as soon as possible.
7. Keep out of crowded houses.

8. **IF YOU DON'T FEEL RIGHT CALL ON YOUR PLANT DOCTOR FOR ADVICE**

WHI IMAGE ID 49032

Pneumonia was a very scary disease. This poster from 1921 told workers how to spot and prevent pneumonia.

Sterling and his family attended Libby's funeral. White flowers surrounded her head as she lay in her casket. They were hyacinths, the same type of flowers Sterling had helped her tend each spring. He had always enjoyed their fragrance because it was one of the earliest signs that a new season had arrived. But after his mother's funeral, that changed. The smell of hyacinths became a reminder of his mother's death and the intense sadness that he felt. Sterling was unable to plant hyacinths or even go near them for the next 50 years.

No one in the North family was prepared for Libby's death. Sterling's brother and sisters had already moved away from home, so Sterling often found himself alone in his grief. He stopped writing and turned to the outdoors and animals for comfort.

In the years that followed his mother's death, Sterling had to grow up quickly. Although his father David loved his son, David did not know how to raise a young boy. Very often David would go out of town for business. Sometimes Sterling's older sisters would return to Edgerton to care for him. But they couldn't stay for very long.

Sometimes Sterling's father would hire housekeepers, but most of them couldn't take the **freewheeling** style of the North household. After all, how many homes had animals of every type roaming freely in and out? There was a dog,

freewheeling (free **whee** ling): not bound by formal rules or guidelines

muskrats, woodchucks, and a crow residing at the North house at one time or another!

Sterling and his father didn't like housekeepers telling them how to live any more than the housekeepers liked the Norths' way of life. Sterling later recalled one housekeeper who "slowly discouraged and eventually drove away all of my beloved pets.... I have forgiven most of my enemies, but she I may never forgive."

Sometimes Sterling was left to fend for himself. Fortunately, it was a time when most of the townspeople knew one another very well. Neighbors kept a watchful eye on Sterling's comings and goings. It was not unusual for Sterling to receive a warm pot of homemade soup or freshly baked cherry pie from a neighbor who worried about his welfare.

When Sterling wasn't at Edgerton Elementary School, he was often outside playing with his friends. The game of marbles was one of their favorite pastimes. The object of the game was to hit as many of your opponent's marbles with your own marble as you could. The largest marble was called the "glassie." It was worth 25 smaller marbles, called "mibs." If you hit the glassie, it was like hitting the jackpot.

Most of the boys carried their winnings of marbles home in little leather pouches for safekeeping. To Sterling's regret, he would always return his winnings to the pile for the others to scramble over when the game was done. He remembered his mother's  words of caution. "If you start playing marbles for 'keeps,' you will soon be pitching for pennies. Finally, you'll end up playing cards for money and betting on the horses out at the Irish Picnic grounds." When Sterling was older, he wrote, "My mother thought gambling was a major social evil. Playing for fun was fine, but not for keeps."

On summer nights, the kids from the neighborhood would gather after supper for team games of "pom-pom-pull-away" or "run, sheep, run." In "pom-pom pull-away," 2 teams faced each other on opposite sides of the road. One person who was "it" would stand between the 2 teams and call out the name of one of the players. That player would try to run to safety on the other side without being tagged. The team that ended up with the smallest number of people tagged won the game.

"Run, sheep, run" was a version of hide-and-seek. One team, called the "foxes," had to find the other team, called the "sheep," who had hidden in the nearest hiding spot. The object of the game was for the sheep to sneak back to their original "sheep pen" without being caught by the foxes.

In June and July the sunlit hours seemed to go on forever. Finally, the chorus of croaking frogs from the nearby marshes signaled that the day was done. Parents would call their children home to bed. When Sterling's father was away on business, Sterling would return to an empty house.

Sterling also used his free time to visit his father's brother Fred and his family. They lived in the North homestead next to the original log cabin. Sterling loved to visit Uncle Fred and

Aunt Lillie's. Their house always smelled of Aunt Lillie's baking bread or homemade cookies. Sterling felt connected to the 3 generations that had preceded him as he sat down to meals at the long wooden table in the kitchen. It was warm and cozy with a wood-burning stove in the middle of the room.

But the biggest attraction of visits to the homestead was the presence of his cousin Ernest.

Many years later, Sterling wrote about his cousin. "Ernest was the cousin closest to me. He was lively and bright and

optimistic." Sterling remembered the hickory nuts that he and Ernest collected, sometimes picking them from the grounds of an unsuspecting

This wood-burning stove warms up a farmhouse kitchen much like the stove at Uncle Fred and Aunt Lillie's house.

farmer. He and Ernest rode the family ponies, named Teddy, Nellie, and Fanny, for hours at a time. They ate fresh honey from the bee hives that Uncle Fred kept. On cold winter days, Sterling and Ernest would use the empty bee crates and abandoned honeycombs to erect elaborate buildings and bridges.

Back in Edgerton, winter held its own outdoor adventures. When Sterling and his friends weren't whizzing down a hill on their Flexible Flyer sleds, they were strapping on ice skates to glide across the frozen surface of Lake Koshkonong. The lake usually froze solid by December. But sometimes the ice was thinner than it looked, and sometimes it

COURTESY OF THE NORTH ARCHIVES

A visit to Cousin Ernest's house where Sterling loved to build with wooden blocks cracked. There were stories about kids who had come across spots that were too thin to support their body weight. Some had fallen into the cold water and drowned.

That didn't stop Sterling and his friends from skating for miles across the ice.

One day, Sterling, his friend Bud Babcock, and the 2 Condon brothers called Big and Little had skated about one and a half miles from shore when Sterling spotted a crack in the ice that revealed a large area of lake water.

"Come on, let's jump across," Sterling said.

The 3 older boys were good jumpers. They had often practiced jumping over

Sterling loved to skate on the frozen lake every winter.

2 or 3 pickle barrels at a time. Only Little Condon hesitated. The older 3 boys mustered their courage and took running leaps across the icy **crevasse**. Little Condon remained behind, on the other side of the split ice.

"You're a chicken-hearted scaredy-cat," Big Condon called to his little brother.

Finally, Little Condon followed the bigger boys' lead. He made it. But he didn't speak to the other boys until they were back on the shore.

Later that day, Big Condon roasted hot dogs over a fire he had made with twigs and branches. When he handed one to his younger brother, Little Condon forced back the tears that had been pent up inside. After wiping his nose on the sleeve of his jacket, he took a bite of his sizzling hot dog and felt a sense of pride at his **accomplishment**. Chances are, none of the boys grew up to think that what they had done was wise. But fortunately, they all lived to tell their tales of daring to future generations.

crevasse (kri **vas**): a crack in ice or rock   accomplishment (uh **kahm** plish muhnt): something successfully done or reached through effort

Winter wasn't all fun and adventure, however. There were many chores to do, such as keeping the wood box filled. As he got a little older, Sterling was responsible for sawing, splitting, and carrying in cords of wood to heat the house and cook the food.

When the snow was too deep for family or neighbors to get out to their barns for milking or to the road for delivering goods to town, Sterling was called to lend a hand at digging out. His grandparents, aunts, and uncles would call a town operator on the hand-cranked telephones that hung on their walls. Most people in town knew the operators by their first names and could recognize their voices. The conversation would go something like this:

"Number, please," the operator would say.

"Oh, it's you, Dorothy," the caller would say. "Well, connect me with the North house. I want Sterling to get right over here and shovel me out."

Although Sterling usually received cookies or a piece of homemade pie for his effort, he remembered a special occasion when he received the large sum of 50¢ from his grandfather North. Sterling might have set out for the Badger Ice Cream shop for a 5¢ ice cream cone. But he had also learned the importance of saving. Sterling made sure to stash most of his reward in the gray earthenware crock

A telephone operator sits at her switchboard.

where he kept his treasures of arrowheads, bird feathers, and particularly beautiful stones.

When the weather allowed, Sterling rode his bicycle everywhere he went. As he grew taller, he began to outgrow his small 2-wheeler and knew it needed to be replaced. One day he spotted a beautiful bike with blue and chrome fenders in the window at the local hardware store. The only problem was that it cost $39, a sum Sterling did not have. He was afraid the bike would be sold to someone else before he had a chance to buy it. So he decided to take his savings to the storekeeper in exchange for a promise that the bike would be set aside until Sterling could purchase it.

One year later, after mowing lawns, selling his fresh catches of catfish, and delivering newspapers, Sterling put the rest of the money on the counter and proudly rode off with his new prize. From then on, Sterling could be seen whizzing past the townspeople, the blue and chrome fenders of his new bike shining as the wheels whirled by.

WHI IMAGE ID 23911

Two children pose with bicycles similar to the one Sterling saved up to buy.

32

6

Rascal to the Rescue

As Sterling grew from a small boy to a preteen with greater responsibilities, other changes were beginning to happen in Edgerton and the rest of the country, as well.

This poster featuring Uncle Sam was used to recruit men into the US Army for World War I.

In the spring of 1917, when Sterling was 10 years old, the first dramatic change occurred. The United States joined the war against Germany. Although World War I had been raging in Europe since 1914, Sterling had been too young and too busy with his boyhood activities to feel its impact.

The only time the war had entered his life was when the neighborhood boys dug trenches and threw clods of dirt in pretend battles.

But in 1917, Sterling's older brother Herschel was sent to fight in some of the fiercest battles of the war. One took place in **Soissons**, France, a place that Sterling couldn't begin to picture in his mind. All Sterling knew was that he missed his brother terribly.

COURTESY OF THE NORTH ARCHIVES

Sterling's brother, Herschel

Sterling had heard enough talk between his father and the other townspeople to know that the emperor of Germany, Kaiser Wilhelm II, was considered the enemy. In Sterling's anger and fear for his brother's life, he took a jack knife and carved the words "Damn Kaiser Bill" across the outside wall of the family's barn. In fact, that barn still stands, and those words can still be seen today.

Soissons: swah **sohn**

The Great War, as it was called at that time, came to Edgerton in big and small ways. Townspeople began their own "war gardens" in a united effort to grow enough food to send to the troops fighting so far away. Sterling began a garden in the backyard on Rollin Street. He was proud of the wax beans, peas, and radishes that he would take to Pringles or Wilson's, the local grocery stores. The money he received for his produce made him realize that his many hours tilling the soil, planting seeds, and tending the garden were worth it.

WHI IMAGE ID 3548

This World War I poster encouraged Americans to grow and preserve vegetables to support the war effort. The poster was produced by the National War Garden Commission.

The community banded together in other ways, too. That fall, school was delayed by a month so that the school children could help harvest the large tobacco crop. Usually the town's young men did this work, but most of them were serving overseas.

The community also collected tin that could be used in the production of military equipment. Neighbors brought their flattened tin cans, scraps of tin foil, and old tools to a central gathering place from where they were sent to the closest war production factory.

A child and her pet crow—much like Sterling and Poe-the-Crow!

belfry (bel free): a tower or room for bells

However, Sterling's pet Poe-the-Crow had other ideas. Crows are known for being attracted to shiny objects. Poe was no different than the rest of his species. He would bring home old keys and abandoned whistles found in the streets or fields in and around Edgerton. Then he would fly up to the church **belfry** next door to the Norths' house to hide his metal treasures.

Although the fighting occurred far away from the United States, the war took a heavy toll on the country's soldiers and their families. Sadly, gold stars began to appear in the windows of townspeople whose loved ones had been killed in battle. Almost 2,000 Wisconsin servicemen and women were killed by the war's end in November 1918.

In July 1918 the people of Edgerton gathered at the Methodist church for the funeral of Rollie Adams. Those who knew Rollie said he had been one of the nicest people at Edgerton High School. People in the church wept as Reverend Hooton talked about Rollie's friendly smile and cheerful greeting. Sterling sat in the church and worried whether his own brother would ever return home.

Fortunately, as the scary thoughts of war were worrying Sterling, Rascal the raccoon entered his life.

One day in May 1918, Sterling, his dog Wowser, and a friend were walking through the woods. Suddenly Wowser began to bark. He pawed furiously at the entrance to an animal's den as Sterling and his friend cheered him on. They were eager to see what the dog would discover under the leaves and dirt.

After several moments of noise and commotion, a mother raccoon jumped out from the den and began to hiss. She ran up the closest tree to defend herself, and then she eventually scampered down to round up her babies and lead them off out of sight. She did not seem to notice that a fourth baby raccoon, or kit, was left behind to fend for himself.

Sterling knew enough about animals to realize he should never handle a little creature in its nest. But he also knew that this young kit would never make it on his own without food. And so, with great excitement, Sterling and his friend decided they would take the helpless creature home to feed and care for it.

The little raccoon was curled up and whimpering. Gingerly, Sterling's friend reached inside the den, careful not to handle the little kit too aggressively. Slowly he **coaxed** the frightened critter out of his hole and into Sterling's cap.

Two small, masked eyes blinked, first at the light of day and then at the 2 boys eyeing him intently. Sterling took the shivering animal into his hands so that the warmth of his own body might assure the little raccoon that he was a friend, not a **foe**.

At first, the 2 boys carried the baby raccoon to Sterling's friend's house. But his friend's father sternly refused to let "that wild animal" inside the house. Sterling's father, however, viewed the world differently, and he often

This raccoon might be what Rascal looked like.

coaxed (kohkst): influenced by gentle urging　**foe**: enemy

seemed too busy to notice what Sterling was up to. So Rascal easily slipped into the North family, becoming Sterling's closest companion at a time when he desperately needed one.

At first Rascal lived in the family barn. But eventually he worked his way into the North family's hearts and home, and even to their dining table and beds. Before long, Rascal's masked eyes became known to nearly everyone in Edgerton. Rascal could be seen peering over the top of Sterling's bike basket as the 2 rode along Fulton Street, the main street in town, to do errands. Often they were sighted on their way to Koshkonong Creek or Indian Ford Dam for a day at their favorite fishing spots.

It didn't take long for Rascal to become more skilled at fishing with his tiny claws than Sterling was with his fishing rod and lure. Rascal would follow Sterling into his war garden by day and crawl in bed to cuddle at night. His soothing presence always seemed to ease Sterling's fears about the war.

It wasn't until Sterling's sister Theo came for a visit that Rascal's presence became a problem. Theo was **appalled** that a furry 4-legged creature had the run of the house. She couldn't believe Rascal was even allowed to sit at the dining room table, where he enjoyed taking sugar cubes from the sugar bowl.

As a **courtesy**, Theo was given Sterling's bedroom when she came to visit her father and younger brother. Since Rascal was a **nocturnal** animal, he would often roam the house while his human family slept. One night Theo awoke suddenly to feel Rascal's furry tail swish across her face. Theo's scream was so loud it could have awakened the sleeping neighbors.

Shortly after Theo was married, she paid another visit to Sterling and her father. This time she proudly wore her new sparkling diamond engagement ring. One morning she woke to find that the ring was gone from the edge of the bathroom sink where she thought she had put it the night before.

appalled (uh **pawld**): shocked, horrified, or disgusted   **courtesy** (**kur** tuh see): a polite or generous act
nocturnal (nok **tur** nuhl): active at night

Sister Theo, whose ring was stolen by Rascal and Poe-the-Crow

Sterling's other sister, Jessica, was a well-respected poet. She had a big influence on Sterling and his future career.

The family searched the house and garden but found no sign of Theo's beautiful ring. Theo was beside herself with loss.

Just when all looked hopeless, Sterling had an idea. He had heard Rascal and Poe-the-Crow making a racket on the porch the night before, but he had been too tired to drag himself from bed to investigate. But Sterling knew both animals were very fond of shiny objects. He began to put the puzzle pieces together. It was possible Rascal had spotted the ring during his nightly excursion through the house. When Poe saw Rascal with the shiny ring, he was probably struck with envy. That was most likely when the 2 began to squawk and tussle, waking Sterling from his deep sleep.

Since Poe was usually the victor in such scraps, Sterling thought the crow might have flown up to the church belfry to deposit his treasure into the pile he had been carefully hoarding away.

Sterling knew what to do. Like a detective who was onto an important lead, he climbed up the 75-foot belfry to search for evidence of the robber's crime. Once Sterling got there, it didn't take him long to find the missing ring shining among the scraps of tin foil, whistles, and keys. Theo was thrilled to have her ring back, but she was quick to give one of her many lectures about getting the animals out of the house.

7

Best Friends at the Fair

The same year the United States entered the war and
Rascal entered Sterling's life, the automobile made a big
splash in Edgerton.

Some of the first automobiles in United States were made
in Wisconsin. In the early days, automobiles were powered
by steam, **kerosene**, or electricity. The very first steam-driven
car was designed and produced by Reverend Dr. J. W. Carhart
in Racine. By 1902, the steam-powered Rambler was made in
Kenosha.

Beginning in 1908, the General Motors car company
soon made enough automobiles to transform daily lives in
big cities. Eventually, the horseless carriage reached rural
Wisconsin, too. But in the country, the roads were muddy,
deeply rutted, and narrow. There were no road signs to tell

kerosene (**ker** uh seen): a thin oil used as a fuel

A Rambler pulls a cart carrying several men.

drivers where they were going. The early automobiles did not have headlights, horns, or roofs. Rural drivers and passengers were in for a windy and **treacherous** ride. They used motor goggles, visor caps, and long top coats called "dusters" to protect themselves from flying debris, rain, or strong winds.

Most people still drove wagons or buggies pulled by horses. Many accidents happened on the country roads when a horse reared at the sight and sound of the strange new vehicle. The government passed strict laws that required automobile drivers to slow down whenever they approached a horse and buggy.

treacherous (**tre** chuh ruhs): not safe because of hidden dangers

The automobile was unpopular among many rural people. Some people called automobiles "devil wagons." Some farmers even put wire or nails on the road to puncture the cars' tires. They thought automobiles were a **nuisance**. Instead, they believed horses, bicycles, motorcycles, and trains were fine for getting around.

A buggy pulled by a team of horses

Sometimes, they would slow their horse-driven wagons and pretend to be deaf to frustrate the automobile driver behind them.

Nowhere was there greater competition between horse-driven wagons and motorized cars than at the Irish Picnic and Horse Fair in Edgerton. People gathered from all over the

nuisance (**noo** suhns): an annoying or troublesome person, thing, or situation

46

area. Women and girls wore bonnets and cotton dresses, and men and boys wore visor caps and knee-length **knickers**.

On the weekend of the fair in 1918, Sterling's father was on a business trip to Montana. So Rascal accompanied Sterling to the fair that year. Sterling couldn't wait to show his friend all the exciting things there were to do and see.

First came the pie-eating contest. Sterling decided to enter since the winner took home a $3 prize. There were 20 blueberry pies, 10 lined up on each side of a long wooden table. Each pie was waiting to be devoured by the 20 boys who entered the contest. With their hands tied behind their backs, each boy would try to be the fastest one to eat the entire pie.

As the starting gun sounded, the boys lowered their faces and began furiously eating the crust and gooey blueberries in front of them. They had no way to keep the pie tins in place, so the tins would slip back and forth on the table, making the task more difficult. Sterling could see that the town bully was gobbling up his pie faster than anyone in the crowd.

knickers: loose-fitting pants that button just below the knee

Sterling wasn't about to let him win. Just as it looked like all was lost, as Sterling recalled, "my best friend Rascal came to my rescue." Rascal loved blueberries. Climbing up on the table, Rascal was happy to do his part. While the town bully stopped eating his

Boys with pie filling on their faces after a pie-eating contest

pie to shout his objections to a raccoon joining the contest, Sterling and Rascal lapped up the remaining pie and easily won.

Although the judges laughed at the spectacle, they knew that it wouldn't be fair for Sterling to win the $3 prize with all the help he had from Rascal. But at least Sterling's 4-footed friend tried to help the best he could.

With Rascal propped on his shoulder, Sterling toured the rest of the grounds. He showed his friend the livestock building, and they rode the merry-go-round and the Ferris wheel.

Finally, the harnessed horse-racing contests were about to start. Proud horse owners spent hours grooming their **Suffolks**, Clydesdales, and **Belgians** to a silky perfection before the races began.

As Sterling and Rascal settled at the side of the ring to watch, there was particular excitement in the air. That year, a local minister challenged Mike Conway and his black stallion, Donnybrook, to a race against the minister's brand new Model T roadster. The crowd expected the minister's new "devil wagon" to leave the horse and buggy far behind. What a surprise when Mike Conway and Donnybrook had already ridden once around the entire ring while the minister was still cranking up his sputtering engine!

Suffolks: suh fuhks   **Belgians: bel** juhnz

49

Once the roadster got going, the excited crowd was in for another shock. The large tires on the Model T were not able to take the sharp curves of the track without skidding and sliding around. They

A Model T Ford

were no match for the sure-footedness of Donnybrook and the thin wooden wheels of Mike Conway's buggy. Much to the delight of many in the crowd, the horse-drawn vehicle still seemed to be a pretty good way to get around, at least on that day at the fair.

Despite the **naysayers**, some people were excited about the automobile's arrival. Sterling's father joined the growing number of auto enthusiasts. He replaced the North's faithful old horse with a new Model T Ford for just over $500.

Sterling knew the motorcar was a sign that times were changing. As it turns out, there were more changes awaiting him than he could have imagined.

naysayer (**nay** say ur): a person who says something will not work or is not possible

8

Freedom and Captivity

Although Sterling didn't spend a lot of time with his father, the times they did spend together seemed magical. The summer day when his father suggested a camping trip to the North Woods of Wisconsin was to be one of the most memorable. This time they would be accompanied by 3-month-old Rascal, who also seemed ready for a new adventure.

There were no wide highways in those days, so the trip in the North's new car was long and wonderful. Rascal sprawled out in the back seat, and Sterling sat in the front seat next to his father. Sterling put on his motor goggles to protect his eyes from any debris that might fly up from the road. He watched the scenery change from **deciduous** maple, oak, and elm trees to stately **conifers** and white-barked birch. They drove past a vast assortment of blue waterways, both

deciduous (di **si** juh wuhs): having parts that fall off at the end of a period of growth **conifer** (**kah** nuh fur): a tree or shrub that produces cones and has leaves that look like needles or scales

large and small. As the familiar scent of southern Wisconsin's moist green fields of corn faded away, the fragrance of pine needles filled the air. It was the first time Sterling and Rascal had ever been outside of the farmland they both had known since birth.

Their final destination was the shore of the Brule River. Once they arrived, Sterling and his father prepared hammocks for sleeping in the open air. But their time together was to be short. After settling in, Sterling's father told him that he needed to serve as an expert witness in a court trial happening in nearby Superior, Wisconsin. Sterling then realized the real reason for the trip.

This postcard shows the Brule River flowing through a forest.

As his father left each day for his duties in court 20 miles away, Sterling and Rascal were left to explore the vast forest or wade in the clear waters of the Brule River. As the 2 free spirits romped through the green canopy of fir trees or splashed in the cold water, there was a sense of bliss they both savored.

After all, Rascal knew what it was like to be confined. A few weeks earlier, Rascal caused a big commotion with a neighbor. The crime rate was very low in Edgerton, so most people in town never locked their doors. On warm summer nights, the North family left their front door wide open to allow breezes to flow through the screen door and into the house. That made it very easy for Rascal to open the light screen door with a push of his front paws.

Once outside, Rascal explored the neighborhood. One night, he discovered the neighbor's cornfield. Rascal liked what he found. He joyfully began to eat, leaving many tall stalks stripped of their plump, ripe ears of corn.

When the neighbor discovered Rascal's crime the next morning, he made angry threats that he would trap or shoot "that animal." He demanded that Rascal wear a collar with a leash if Sterling wanted to save his pet's life. Even worse, Rascal now needed to be caged at night, or else!

Rascal loved to eat corn from cornfields.

Sterling could hardly bear the thought of putting his friend through such a shameful punishment, but he knew it was better than the neighbor's threats of harm. Sadly, Sterling built a cage and bought a colorful collar and leash.

But along the Brule River, the 2 were free to run in the great outdoors, with no cage and no school bell. Sterling thought he could live in such a sun-filtered place for the rest of his life. He believed Rascal felt the same way.

Before he fell asleep, Sterling would stare up at the summer sky with its thousands of bright stars. It's possible those moments were the happiest he could remember since the sadness of losing his mother 4 years earlier.

That fall, Sterling began the sixth grade. The start of the school year filled Sterling with curiosity. What interesting facts would he write down in the pages of his new notebook?

It was the beginning of a very memorable year, when Sterling met 2 of his favorite teachers. Miss Whalen loved to teach about the wonders of plants and animals in her biology room. And Miss Stafford made the written word come alive in English class. Not surprisingly, biology and English were Sterling's 2 favorite subjects. They were the same subjects Sterling's mother introduced him to when he was a little boy.

Sterling's school year was off to a good start. But to his dismay, this was the beginning of a tough time for Rascal.

One day, Miss Whalen invited her students to bring their favorite pets to school. When it was Sterling's turn to share, he brought Rascal. All went well until the class bully pulled his rubber-band slingshot from his pocket and aimed for Rascal's nose. Rascal, who had always been treated with love and respect, screeched in shock and anger from the blow. As any hurt raccoon might do, Rascal nipped the boy's hand in self-defense.

Because raccoons can carry **rabies**, Miss Whalen had no choice but to tell Sterling to keep Rascal caged for the next 14 days. It was the only way to make sure Rascal was free of the disease.

It was bad enough that Rascal had to be caged at night after his encounter with the neighbor's corn field. But when Rascal needed to be kept in the cage for 2 weeks, 24 hours a day, it was more than Sterling could stand. Sterling knew what it was like to feel lonely and alone. So each day, he would come home from school and crawl into the cage beside his furry friend to talk and share special snacks. Those 2 weeks probably felt like the longest in young Sterling's life.

rabies: a deadly disease of the nervous system that affects animals and can be passed on to people by the bite of an infected animal

9

The Flu Pandemic Hits Home

Sterling was still waiting for his brother to return home from war. He needed to keep himself busy, so he decided to build a canoe in the middle of the living room. The wooden boat was 18 feet long and 28 inches wide. It filled most of the room! Sterling's sister Theo could not stand the fact that the once neatly decorated parlor was now covered with tools and wood shavings. And yet Sterling and his father hardly noticed the disturbance.

Building the canoe occupied many hours of Sterling's time and attention that year. It was a perfect distraction from the thoughts of war and worry about his brother. Sterling needed to solve many problems to make the vessel water-worthy. He solved one such problem by collecting old cheese crates from every store in town. Their **cylindrical** shape would

cylindrical (suh **lin** dri kuhl): having a long round shape

provide the perfect rigs of support for the bow-shaped canoe that would one day become his favorite means of transportation.

COURTESY OF THE NORTH ARCHIVES

Sterling built this canoe at age 12.

Unfortunately, his building project was interrupted in late October 1918. That fall, the Spanish **influenza pandemic** hit southern Wisconsin like a tornado. More people in Wisconsin died of the flu that year than had died in the war.

Sterling was very disappointed when his school closed to help stop the spread of the deadly virus. People who ventured out of their homes wore white gauze masks over their noses and mouths.

influenza: in floo **en** zuh   **pandemic** (pan **de** mik): an occurrence in which a disease spreads very quickly and affects a large number of people over a wide area

58

Spanish Influenza

Although influenza spread throughout the world, it was known as the Spanish flu because it was first reported in Spain. Many countries fighting in World War I were restricted in what they could report in their newspapers. But Spain did not take sides during World War I. So news of the flu outbreak was reported freely in its newspapers.

The war, however, helped spread the illness, as servicemen from all over the world brought it back to their homelands.

Home remedies such as eating onions at every meal, putting salt in the nostrils, or inhaling smoke from hot coals were some of the methods falsely claimed to be a cure.

In Wisconsin, people who had the flu were **quarantined** in their homes. Many public activities were closed. The Spanish flu pandemic lasted from January 1918 to December 1920. More than 8,000 Wisconsin residents died of Spanish influenza during this time. Almost 50 million people died worldwide.

quarantined (**kwawr** uhn teend): separated from other people to prevent the spread of disease

When headache and fever gripped Sterling one night, his father decided that his son needed more care than he was able to give with his frequent business trips. So off they went to Aunt Lillie and Uncle Fred's house, with Rascal sitting beside Sterling to make sure that everything was going to be all right. Fortunately, Sterling had only a mild case of the frightening disease that had already killed several neighbors.

As always, Aunt Lillie and Uncle Fred welcomed Sterling and Rascal into their home. They cleared the room right next to theirs so that Aunt Lillie could watch over Sterling day and night. She would often read to Sterling by the kerosene lamp that served as the major source of light in their old farmhouse.

Sometimes Sterling would listen to the new Edison talking machine that sat in the parlor. He enjoyed cranking it up and watching the shiny black **cylinder** rotate around as the sharp, needlelike **stylus** made contact with each of its turns. How amazing it seemed to hear a favorite song spill forth from the large wooden box until the rotation stopped.

cylinder: **si** luhn dur   **stylus** (**stɪ** luhs): a very small, pointed piece of metal that touches a record and produces sound when the record is played

60

Two children sit on a porch with an Edison Standard phonograph.

Edison Talking Machine

Thomas Edison invented the first talking machine in 1877. His machine was more like a voice recorder than a phonograph. Although people were amazed by the new machine, it was used mainly in businesses for people to dictate notes.

In the early 1900s, Edison invented a new form of talking machine that could play music. After it was hand cranked, a **horizontal** cylinder rotated around, and the stylus made contact with the grooves to create sound. At first the music lasted only about 2 minutes, or as long as it took the stylus to get from one end of the cylinder to the other. In 1908, Edison devised a new cylinder with finer grooves that would allow the music to play twice as long.

WHI IMAGE ID 9585

Thomas Edison in his lab

By 1912, Edison came out with the Blue **Amberol** record, a flat disc made of unbreakable **celluloid** that created much better sound than the cylinder. From Edison's early invention came the flat celluloid and vinyl records that became popular in the late 1940s, 1950s, and 1960s. Today, many people still use record players in their homes. Maybe your grandparents still have records and a record player. Have you ever seen them?

horizontal (hor uh **zahn** tuhl): lying flat or level   **Amberol:** am bur awl   **celluloid:** plastic used to make film and records

In the past when Sterling had **croup**, a bit of kerosene on a sugar cube would have been a common remedy. But with the flu, rest and time were the only known treatments. As the days passed, Sterling began feeling stronger and stronger. By early November, he was well enough to join the family for dinner at the table. Aunt Lillie made a turkey dinner complete with hickory-nut dressing and freshly baked **mince** pie.

That night, Sterling's father drove out to the farm to collect the recovered patient and his ring-tailed friend. As they all sat down to the dinner table, Aunt Lillie suddenly realized that it was the fourth day of November. Until then, not even Sterling's father had remembered that it was Sterling's birthday. Aunt Lillie apologized that she hadn't made Sterling a cake and led everyone in singing "Happy Birthday." But surviving the deadly flu was an even better birthday gift.

croup (kroop): a throat condition, usually occurring in children, that causes a barking cough   **mince**: mins

10

Cheers and Tears

Shortly after Sterling returned home from Aunt Lillie and Uncle Fred's, he received the best birthday gift of all. The United States and its **allies** defeated their enemies in World War I. **Armistice Day** was declared on November 11, 1918. Towns and cities hung banners and held parades as happy families gathered at train stations to welcome their soldiers home. Sterling's brother Herschel was one of the lucky young men who came home unharmed.

Edgerton was decorated with flags and banners that celebrated the country's victory. Sterling wanted to be part of the celebration. So he decorated his bicycle spokes with red, white, and blue crepe paper. Rascal hopped in the bike basket, and together they rode down Edgerton's main street. Sterling rang the bell on his handlebars as loud as he could. This was the day he had been hoping for.

ally (a lı): a person, group, or nation united with another in a common purpose **Armistice** (ahr muh stuhs) **Day**: the day on which the countries involved in World War I signed an agreement to stop fighting

WHI IMAGE ID 1953

A parade celebrates the end of World War I on November 11, 1918.

After the festivities, Sterling and Rascal returned to their daily routines. Rascal settled back in as a regular resident on Rollin Street, despite the concerns of some neighbors who watched him grow larger and larger.

As the fall shifted to winter, Sterling could see that Rascal was getting very tired. Although raccoons do not **hibernate**,

hibernate (**hı** bur nayt): pass all or part of the winter in an inactive state in which body temperature drops and breathing slows

they do sleep a lot during the cold winter days. Rascal decided to take his daily naps in the hole of a big tree in Sterling's back yard. Sterling took one of his warmest wool sweaters and lined Rascal's den so that his friend would be as comfortable as possible when the temperatures got down to freezing.

When spring finally arrived, Sterling realized that it had been nearly one year since he had found his favorite companion. By now, Rascal had grown from a small, furry creature that could be held in one hand to a full-grown, 20-pound male raccoon.

One night, as a spring breeze drifted through Sterling's open bedroom window, he heard a female raccoon making a soft crooning sound nearby. Rascal immediately called back from the **confines** of his small cage.

confines: boundary or limit

66

The next night, Rascal learned to unlock the hook that closed his cage and went out to explore a neighbor's henhouse. The loud ruckus of the hens squawking could be heard throughout the neighborhood. Sterling knew Rascal's life would be at risk if he ever tried anything like that again.

With great regret, Sterling realized that he would soon have to allow his friend to choose how

COURTESY OF WALTER DIEDRICK

An artist's interpretation shows Rascal and Sterling fishing at Indian Ford.

he wanted to live the rest of his life. Would Rascal want to remain a pet? Or would he want to be set free in the wild, where raccoons are supposed to live?

By the time April was nearing its end, Sterling knew it was time to do one of the hardest things he had ever done. On a warm Saturday afternoon, he and Rascal set out in the canoe, as they had so many times before. Only this time it was different.

With sadness, Sterling paddled toward the marshy shore of Koshkonong Creek, near the outskirts of town. There he would let his best friend decide what to do.

Sterling thought that Rascal seemed to sense the importance of the moment. When they reached the shallow water of the creek's bank, Sterling set his paddle aside and sat silently next to his friend. The low light of dusk hung over the wild forest ahead, soon replaced by the light of the moon. Sterling later recalled that for several moments Rascal listened to the sounds of the forest calling to him. Then he jumped from his familiar spot inside the canoe and landed in the shallow water. Confidently, Rascal climbed onto the shore.

As Sterling watched, he saw Rascal disappear into the trees. Only once did the raccoon look back, as if to say good-bye and thank you to his friend. As Sterling watched Rascal go, he felt a deep sorrow in his heart. Still, he knew Rascal had made the right decision.

Although Sterling would never see Rascal again, he knew that he would never forget their picnics of shared strawberry jelly sandwiches. He would always remember the moments they sat together in the crook of a tree. And above all, Sterling would always be grateful to Rascal for being his friend during his loneliest time.

11
Unexpected Growing Pains

Sterling spent much of his childhood canoeing, fishing, and hunting wild game for dinner. But in 1920, his entry into Edgerton High School brought about other interests. As a freshman, Sterling's slim body was becoming stronger and more muscular. He dreamed of being on the school's boxing, track, and football teams. He had already been to an overnight summer camp where he set records in the 100-yard dash, broad jump, and high jump. Sterling was very proud of his athletic accomplishments and collected all the ribbons he earned in a notebook in his bedroom.

As Sterling grew bigger, so did the jobs he took on to earn money. The summer after his sophomore year, Sterling lived and worked on a farm owned by Nellie Tibert, halfway between Edgerton and nearby Stoughton. His days started at

WHI IMAGE ID 30875

Edgerton High School

4:00 a.m. First he milked the cows and cleaned the stalls. Then he helped hoe and **cultivate** the 30 acres of tobacco.

After the morning chores were done, Sterling set to work clearing large tree stumps and granite boulders that weighed up to 2 tons. The stumps and boulders had been carried along with the glacial ice sheets that began to move across parts of Wisconsin more than 150,000 years ago. The sheets of ice deposited debris as they traveled across the rich soil of southern Wisconsin.

cultivate (**kuhl** tuh vayt): raise or assist the growth of crops by tilling or labor

71

WHI IMAGE ID 75518

Working on a farm could be dangerous. Here, a farmer stands at the edge of a wooden wagon, pitching hay into a thresher.

Tractors were rare when Sterling worked on the farm, so the only way to clear the stumps and solid rock was to first blast them into smaller pieces by using dynamite.

In return for his labor, Sterling was given 6¢ an hour, good home-cooked meals, and a very small room with a window that overlooked the barn.

It was 1922, the year the farm **depression** began. The price of land and crops **plummeted** all over the country. Farmers were able to sell fewer crops. And the crops they did sell were worth less money. The depression affected the many acres in Montana that Sterling's father owned. Sterling knew he would need to earn his own money for anything he wanted since his father's wealth was once again gone.

During the August **threshing** season, no day was complete without pitching hay, stacking bundles of wheat into neat piles, and carrying heavy bags of grain to the wagons that would haul them into town. On one very hot day, Sterling began to ache violently while carrying a 100-pound bag of wheat. He wanted to go on with his work but couldn't. Instead, the pain forced him to go inside.

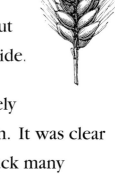

Two days later, Sterling was almost completely **paralyzed** below the waist. He was in great pain. It was clear that he had contracted polio, a disease that struck many children at the time.

depression (di **presh** uhn): period of low activity in business   **plummeted** (**pluh** muh tid): fell straight down
threshing: separating the seed from a harvested plant by beating   **paralyzed** (**per** uh lızd): unable to move all or part of the body

Polio

When Sterling was a little boy, children spent summers swimming at the local swimming hole. But as more and more children were getting polio, parents became frightened and kept their children at home. In Sterling's time, no one knew how children caught the disease, but people believed it was passed from person to person as they gathered in crowded places. Sometimes schools, beaches, and movie theatres closed. Today we know the disease is spread by oral contact with the virus.

The polio virus attacks the nerves that help the muscles move. Often arms, legs, and the **diaphragm** became paralyzed or weakened. Some people were put in leg braces, others in a machine called an iron lung. The iron lung would push and release against the patient's chest to allow him or her to breathe.

WHI IMAGE ID 86713

Franklin D. Roosevelt was the thirty-second president of the United States.

In the early 1920s, polio began to appear all over the country. Adults could get polio, too. In 1921, a man named Franklin Delano Roosevelt contracted polio at the age of 39. Twelve years later, he became the thirty-second president of the United States. President Roosevelt founded an organization to fight polio. It was called the March of Dimes.

diaphragm: the muscle that allows lungs to inhale and exhale

74

Adults and children saved their dimes, placed them in slots on a cardboard card, and donated them with the hope that their money could help fund a cure for polio.

In 1949, Dr. Jonas Salk invented the first vaccine against polio. By 1955, the vaccine was used all over the country. A second vaccine, discovered by the medical scientist Albert **Sabin**, later replaced Dr. Salk's vaccine because it could be given more quickly. Children would line up in the school nurse's room or doctor's office to have a drop of vaccine put on their tongues or on a sugar cube. By 1994, polio was wiped out in nearly every country in the world.

A toddler places a coin into a March of Dimes collection board. The collection helped raise money to cure polio.

A doctor unloads a box filled with the polio vaccine.

Sabin: **say** bin

Doctors didn't know much about polio in 1922. But they told Sterling he would probably never walk again. Sterling, however, was determined. He promised himself that he would not only walk, but he would run, jump, ski, dive from the highest bridge, and climb the tallest trees.

So Sterling set about recovering. After spending months in a wheelchair and on crutches, Sterling was given a 25-pound iron brace that he wore on his right leg for one year. The brace was very heavy, but Sterling forced himself to swim at least one mile every day. He also built an exercise machine made of wooden weights, ropes, and pulleys that he used regularly.

The muscles on his right leg would never return to full strength and left him with a slight limp. But the rest of his body became stronger than ever. Sterling was so pleased with his progress that he submitted his photograph to a body-building contest. He posed in such a way that his right leg was hidden behind his left so no one would see its withered appearance.

Sterling also found comfort in the written word. It was the first time he used his young writing talents since his mother's death 8 years earlier.

Sterling began writing short stories and poetry for *The Crimson*, Edgerton High School's yearbook. He even sold a few poems to national magazines. Much of what he wrote came from his own experiences in the outdoors as a young boy. The first and last verses of a poem that appeared in the *Crimson* provide a good example:

Muskrat and the Moon

From the reedy shore a muskrat slipped,
through the willows crept the moon.
And I asked the wind, the gossiping wind,
the interlacing April wind,
to sing to me a tune.

So now from the shore the muskrat slips,
to meet the rising moon.
and he dives for roots, for sweet white roots,
for arrow-head and lily-roots,
and listens to the loon,
the laughing of the loon.

Earlier that summer, another change happened in Sterling's life almost as unexpectedly as polio. On a Saturday afternoon in June, Sterling walked to the local post office to pick up the mail. He saw a scruffy little dog waiting for someone to open the post office door. Sterling knew every pet in the neighborhood, but he had never seen this dog before.

As Sterling unlocked his post office box, he saw the postmaster place 3 letters and a newspaper into the little dog's soft jaws. The well-trained pup slipped back through the opened door and scampered onto the seat of a waiting car. Sterling noticed the teenage girl sitting next to the driver and realized she was new to town. There was something about her black, shiny hair and friendly face that made Sterling's heart pump a little faster. He had never been interested in girls before, but he later wrote of that day: "June 17th, 1922, was to be the turning point in my life."

The teenage girl sitting on the passenger seat was Gladys Delores Buchanan. Gladys had just moved from Indianapolis, Indiana, with her family and her dog Rags.

From that day at the post office, Gladys brought out Sterling's romantic side. Maybe that's why he decided it would be a good idea to paddle Gladys to the high school senior picnic in the canoe he had built in his living room when he was 12.

Gladys, Sterling's first and only love

The waves on the lake were rough that day. Sterling's friends stood on the shore, shouting directions and waving their arms as the wobbly vessel came closer to the picnic grounds. Gladys and Sterling finally made it, but they were soaked from the rocky voyage. Many years later, in a letter to his boyhood friend Royal Ladd, Sterling remembered that day and admitted, "She did risk her life by letting me paddle her to the senior picnic in that pencil slim craft."

Sterling never joined the high school football team as he'd once dreamed. Instead, his strength was acknowledged in a different way. On page 61 of his senior class yearbook, Sterling's portrait appears with the title, "Not Self but Service." The entire student body had voted Sterling the "strongest all around boy or girl in the high school." The student who received this honor needed to be "courteous, loyal, ambitious, enthusiastic, honest, friendly, and possess superior scholarship."

COURTESY OF THE NORTH ARCHIVES

In the yearbook, each senior was asked to list their greatest weakness. Sterling confessed that his was, "arguing with girls." His greatest **ambition**? "To become a great poet."

Sterling's high school yearbook photo was printed with the caption "Sterling is sterling."

ambition (am **bish** uhn): a thing a person hopes to do or achieve

12

Chicago, Here I Come

Sterling and Gladys dreamed of one day owning a small log cabin of their own. It would be near water and have a beautiful view. First though, Sterling and Gladys needed to go to college.

With one pair of flannel trousers, a gray sweater, and tremendous excitement, Sterling headed off to the University of Chicago to study English.

Going to college introduced Sterling to exciting new opportunities. He joined the Poetry Club of Chicago, where he met other gifted poets. His poems appeared in magazines and received awards. He wrote lyrics for the university's musical comedies. And, as a freshman, he sold his first short story to *Dial Magazine*.

Gladys attended Whitewater College in Wisconsin and graduated in 1926. The next summer, on June 23, she and Sterling were married. It was an exciting time for both of them! Two years later, Sterling's first book, *Pedro Gorino*, was published, and his first child, David, was born on the same day.

WHI IMAGE ID 83023

An elevated view of Chicago's business district and skyline. Sterling wrote about Chicago in many of his articles.

Sterling decided he needed to earn more money to support his young family. In 1929, he left college before graduating and began to write as a reporter for the *Chicago Daily News*. Sterling worked in the same office as the famous poet Carl Sandburg, whom he had greatly admired as a boy. This began Sterling's long career as an author, editor, and **literary critic**. In fact, Sterling was the youngest literary editor ever to work at the newspaper.

literary critic: someone who studies, explains, and judges pieces of writing

82

Sterling would work at the newspaper for 14 years. But he and Gladys missed the countryside of their childhoods. "Very deep in our hearts we were country people," Sterling wrote. "What is bred in the bone cannot be supplanted by any amount of sophistication or success in a career."

With such feelings in their hearts, Sterling and Gladys purchased 25 acres of farmland in nearby Michigan. By that time, they had 2 young children: David, who was 6 years old, and Arielle, who was 3. Their farmland was only 75 miles outside of Chicago. It was the perfect summer retreat for their family.

COURTESY OF THE NORTH ARCHIVES, PHOTOGRAPH BY STERLING NORTH

Gladys, Arielle, and David relaxing at their country home in Michigan

"The clean air of Michigan differs from the smoke and fog of Chicago no less than the clear water of a trout stream differs from the polluted and sluggish fluid of the Chicago River," Sterling wrote.

On the farm, the family lived "by lamplight because the electricity is still far down the road. We have spent 6 blessed seasons without a telephone. We are 2 **merciful** miles from the nearest concrete highway."

Although the Norths thrived on their rural lifestyle in the summer, Sterling never stopped writing. He worked at the newspaper during the day, and he wrote his own novels at night and on Sundays.

After his first novel was published, Sterling thought he would have good luck getting published again. But he was wrong. He

Sterling passed on the lessons of nature to his children, just as his mother had done for him.

merciful (**mur** si fuhl): having compassion or showing kind treatment

84

watched as his next 2 novels were rejected by **publishers**. But Sterling didn't give up. In 1934, his next novel, titled *Plowing on Sunday*, was accepted by the MacMillan Company, a famous publishing house.

Plowing on Sunday was a popular novel with many people across the United States. But most people in and around Edgerton hated it! The story was based on the lives of people in small-town Wisconsin during the days of the 1920s alcohol **prohibition**. Although the names of the characters were changed, many people in Edgerton recognized themselves in the stories and scandals Sterling wrote about in his book. They were so unhappy that the Edgerton librarian refused to put the book on the shelf. Sterling's own uncle, Thomas W. North, was a minister at a nearby church. He led a group in burning every copy of the book they could get their hands on.

Despite the town's furor, Sterling's father sent Sterling this letter of support: "I shall always need you and watch with pride every success you achieve. . . . I have only one present I can make you—the sincere love of an old man."

publisher (**pub** lish ur): a person or company that prepares printed works, like books, for sale   **prohibition** (proh huh **bish** uhn): a law or order that stops something from being used or done

13
Remembering Rascal

Sterling's new recognition as a writer rocketed him and his family all the way to New York City. By the time Sterling flew from Chicago to New York, passenger airplanes were just starting to become common. At age 37, Sterling took his first ride on an airplane, and he loved it. "Flying is one of ... the deepest and most joyous satisfactions I have ever known," he wrote. "Nothing on this earth or in heaven could be so beautiful as America from 9000 feet."

Sterling would continue his writing

WHI IMAGE ID 12140

This Northwest Airlines propeller plane from 1948 is very similar to the plane Sterling would have flown on for the first time.

career in New York City. There was no dispute over his next novel, published in 1947. Everyone loved it. The story about a young boy and his lamb was called *So Dear to My Heart*. It became so popular that Walt Disney Productions turned it into a movie. Audiences all over the world watched the movie and cheered. The story launched Sterling North on a path to literary fame.

For the next 9 years Sterling worked as an editor for the *New York Post* and the *World Telegram* newspapers. New York City was the largest city in the country. It was full of tall buildings and loud city sounds. And once again, Sterling and Gladys longed for a more rural life.

This time they found their escape on a 27-acre plot of land near Morristown, New Jersey. There, they could watch the changing seasons and live surrounded by the natural world.

Just as young Sterling was inspired by nature as he learned from his mother, the adult Sterling was inspired by nature, too. He wrote about it in one of his books, titled *Hurry Spring*.

"Early in March, even before all the snow has melted, Spring begins to ask questions," he wrote. "Usually by the 15th of March the red-winged black birds and the wood ducks have returned to our lake above the waterfall in our enchanted valley near Morristown, New Jersey. They will stay all summer and nest here."

The North home in New Jersey

COURTESY OF THE NORTH ARCHIVES; PHOTOGRAPH BY STERLING NORTH

Sterling was happy. He had found a way to combine his love of nature with his passion for writing. He and Gladys lived on their beautiful land while he continued working for newspapers in the city. He worked very hard. He wrote articles for popular magazines. He wrote a column that was published in newspapers all over the country. And he wrote nearly one novel every year!

But the fast pace eventually wore on his health. Overworked and tired, Sterling retired from the newspaper in 1956 at the age of 50.

Gladys and Sterling in their study at home. Gladys often served as Sterling's editor.

Retirement didn't mean doing nothing! Sterling immediately began to work on a series of books for children called the North Star. The books helped kids all over the country learn about famous people such as Abraham Lincoln, Thomas Edison, and Mark Twain.

He also created a radio program called *Books on Trial*. Every Monday night, 2 literary critics would make a case either for or against a particular book. Sterling acted as the judge. He **presided** over their argument and came up with the final **verdict** in the case.

Home computers didn't exist in the early 1960s. Instead, Sterling wrote his novels on a typewriter. In 1962, he bought a new Underwood typewriter. Maybe he knew he was about to write his twenty-eighth and most beloved story just a month later.

Sterling had come a long way from his childhood in rural Wisconsin, living in a big house full of wild animals for pets. But he never forgot those early days in Edgerton. At age 56, Sterling began to think back to his childhood and what he had learned. He decided other people might be able to learn something if he wrote about how he grew up.

presided: was in charge   **verdict**: a decision reached by a jury or judge

Sterling writing at his typewriter in the family's country home

And so, in 1963, Sterling wrote the story that would be loved by children all over the world. It was called *Rascal: A Memoir of a Better Era*. It would become his most well-known **achievement**.

Rascal told the story of Sterling's year with his beloved pet raccoon. The book was an instant hit. Posters of Sterling

achievement (uh **cheev** muhnt): a thing gotten by great effort

and Rascal hung on the walls of libraries and schools all over the United States. Rascal was a bestseller for 6 months, it won a Newbery Medal, and it received a Young Reader's Choice Award in 1966. It was even **translated** into more than 20 different languages!

Sterling's memoir was so loved that Walt Disney Productions made a movie of the book in 1969. It was simply titled *Rascal*. The movie was shown in theaters all over the world, and figurines of Rascal were sold in places like Japan. Sterling North had become **internationally** famous.

The story about the importance of friendship between a boy and his gentle pet seemed to resonate with readers of all ages. Sterling received many letters from children and adults telling him how much they loved his book. Some of the letter writers even mentioned they had recently acquired a pet raccoon who just happened to be named—you guessed it!—Rascal.

In the book, Sterling changed the name of the town from Edgerton to the fictitious name of **Brailsford** Junction. Brailsford was his maternal grandmother's maiden name. But

translated (**trans** lay tid): turned from one language into another   **internationally** (in tur **nash** uh nuh lee): active or known in many nations   **Brailsford**: braylz ford

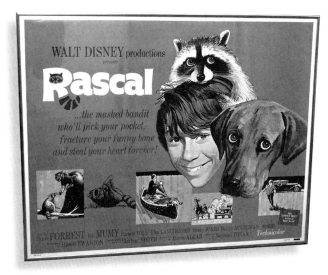

These posters for the movie *Rascal* are on display at the Sterling North Museum in Edgerton.

his old friends and neighbors had no doubt that Sterling was recalling the days of his youth in Edgerton.

The people of Edgerton celebrated Sterling's accomplishments. On Sunday, July 26, 1964, they gathered at the Albion Museum to honor him. Sterling sadly could not be there. Instead, he wrote them a message titled, *A Letter to the People of My Home Town*. In the letter, Sterling apologized for not being able to attend the event. He explained he was meeting with the Disney filmmakers instead, making sure "our region and my family and friends will all be portrayed with the greatest possible **authenticity**."

He ended the letter by saying, "Please remember that I will never forget that without this region, without this **heritage**, without you all, I never could have written *RASCAL*."

COURTESY OF THE STERLING NORTH SOCIETY

Today, visitors to the Sterling North Museum can see different copies of *Rascal: A Memoir of a Better Era*, as well as Sterling North's own typewriter and desk.

authenticity (aw then **ti** suh tee): quality of being true and correct   **heritage** (**her** uh tij): the traditions, achievements, and beliefs that are part of the history of a group of people

14

Sterling North's Legacy

After *Rascal*, Sterling wrote one last book, called *The Wolfling*, in 1969. By this time, Sterling had suffered several strokes. His body was weak and partially paralyzed. This meant he had to type the entire book with only one finger.

Even with his physical limitations, Sterling was able to tell the beautiful story of a young boy who befriended a wolf. The story was based on his father's friendship with the naturalist Theodore Thure Kumlien in the 1870s. The book won the 1969 Dutton Animal Book Award.

Both of Sterling and Gladys's children grew up to become writers, too. Sterling's son David moved to Washington, DC, in the early 1960s, where he was a writer for the government. David remembers his father teaching him about trees, birds, and stars as he was growing up. The family's summer retreat

Wolfling: wulf ling

The Sterling North family: David, Gladys, Sterling, and Arielle

in Michigan taught David how to live simply in the natural world. "The worst part of returning back to the city was having to put on shoes," David said.

Sterling's daughter, Arielle North Olson, became a successful children's book writer and poet. What Arielle remembers most about her father is "the love and encouragement he gave to me and my brother."

96

Even though Sterling and Gladys were happy in their rural home in New Jersey, they never forgot their roots in the Midwest. On July 30, 1964, Sterling wrote to his hometown newspaper, the *Edgerton Reporter*:

"I wish I never had to say goodbye to Wisconsin. In fact, I will always be living there, in my memory. I wish never to say goodbye to the deep pool below the dam at Indian Ford where I waited with excitement night after night for a big catfish to take my bait, reeling them in against the swift current.

"I hope always to remember Wisconsin springtime, from the first breaking of the ice with **thunderous** roars across the miles of lakes and rivers, to the blossoming of shooting stars and violets and wild crabapples over the hills and valleys of my native land."

thunderous (**thun** duh ruhs): very loud

Sterling North died in 1974 at the age of 68. Gladys followed him in 1989 at the age of 81. Just as Sterling wanted to remember his native home, the people of Edgerton wanted to remember him. In 1984, the children of Rock County built a sign in front of the North home on Rollin Street that read, "In this home in 1918, 11-year-old Sterling North lived with his 'ringtailed' wonder pet raccoon Rascal."

The sign in front of Sterling's childhood home

In 1989, residents of Edgerton created the Sterling North Society to preserve the works of one of its most famous residents. In 1992, the society purchased the home on Rollin Street after raising money from **donations** large and small.

Volunteers worked for 12,500 hours to restore the home to its original early-1900s style. On a spring day in 1995, more than 100 third graders from Edgerton Community Elementary School gathered at the Rollin Street home to plant trees around the property. The home opened to the public in 1997.

Today, visitors to the home can see photos, letters, posters, and the typewriter Sterling used to write *Rascal*. The canoe that he built at the age of 12 was on display in the nearby Albion Museum, but it was destroyed in a fire in 1965. Fortunately, one paddle was rescued and is now housed at the Sterling North Society home.

Late in his life, Sterling was asked to give his advice to children. This is what he said:

donation: something given to help those in need

COURTESY OF THE STERLING NORTH SOCIETY

This is what Sterling's house on Rollin Street looks like today.

"My suggestion to young people: Have faith in the future, be kind to animals and each other, and read at least 2 good books a week. Humanity is not yet doomed if we all work toward a better, kinder world."

Sterling North's **legacy** lives on in the 34 books, numerous articles, book reviews, and poems that he has left behind. It lives on in the lives of family and friends who knew and

legacy: something (like memories or knowledge) that comes from the past or a person of the past

loved him. And it will be remembered forever in the minds of readers who continue to be touched by his words.

What would you like to do to make the world a better, kinder place?

Appendix

Sterling North's Time Line

1906 — Thomas Sterling North is born on November 4.

1914 — Sterling's mother Libby dies of pneumonia.

1917 — Sterling's brother Herschel is sent to France to serve in World War I.

1918 — Sterling meets Rascal at a time when he needs a friend.

1919 — Sterling releases Rascal in the wild, and the 2 friends say good-bye.

1922 — Sterling comes down with polio.

1925 — Sterling graduates from Edgerton High School.

1925 — Sterling goes to college at the University of Chicago.

1927 — Sterling marries Gladys Buchanan on June 23.

1929 — The Norths' first child, David, is born, and Sterling's first novel, Pedro Gorino, is published.

1929–1943 — Sterling works as a reporter and, later, literary editor of Chicago Daily News.

1932 — The Norths' second child, Arielle, is born.

1934 — Sterling's hit novel, Plowing on Sunday, is published.

1943 — Sterling moves to New York and begins working for the New York Post as literary editor.

1947 — Sterling's novel So Dear to My Heart is published. The book is made into a Walt Disney Productions movie.

1956 — Sterling retires from newspaper work. He writes several biographies for the Houghton Mifflin Company's North Star series.

1963 — Sterling publishes Rascal: A Memoir of a Better Era. The book receives a Newberry Honor one year later.

1969 — Walt Disney Productions makes Rascal into a movie.

Sterling's final book, The Wolfling, is published.

1974 — Sterling dies at the age of 68 on December 21.

Glossary

Pronunciation Key

a   cat (kat), plaid (plad),
       half (haf)

ah father (**fah** THur),
       heart (hahrt)

air carry (**kair** ee), bear (bair),
       where (whair)

aw all (awl), law (law),
       bought (bawt)

ay say (say), break (brayk),
       vein (vayn)

e   bet (bet), says (sez),
       deaf (def)

ee bee (bee), team (teem),
       fear (feer)

i   bit (bit), women (**wim** uhn),
       build (bild)

ɪ   ice (ɪs), lie (lɪ), sky (skɪ)

o   hot (hot), watch (wotch)

oh open (**oh** puhn), sew (soh)

oi boil (boil), boy (boi)

oo pool (pool), move (moov),
       shoe (shoo)

or order (**or** dur), more (mor)

ou house (hous), now (nou)

u   good (gud), should (shud)

uh cup (kuhp), flood (fluhd),
       button (**buht** uhn)

ur burn (burn), pearl (purl),
       bird (burd)

yoo use (yooz), few (fyoo),
       view (vyoo)

hw what (hwuht), when (hwen)

TH that (THat), breathe (breeTH)

zh measure (**mezh** ur),
       garage (guh **razh**)

104

abandoned (uh **ban** duhnd): left and never returned to

accomplishment (uh **kahm** plish muhnt): something successfully done or reached through effort

achievement (uh **cheev** muhnt): a thing gotten by great effort

ally (**a** lı): a person, group, or nation united with another in a common purpose

ambition (am **bish** uhn): a thing a person hopes to do or achieve

anemone (uh **nem** uh nee): a plant that blooms in spring and has large white or colored flowers

appalled (uh **pawld**): shocked, horrified, or disgusted

Armistice (**ahr** muh stuhs) **Day**: the day on which the countries involved in World War I signed an agreement to stop fighting

authenticity (aw then **ti** suh tee): quality of being true and correct

baffled (**ba** fuhld): completely confused

barreling: moving at a high speed

belfry (**bel** free): a tower or room for bells

biology (bı **ah** luh jee): a science that deals with things that are alive, such as plants and animals

celluloid: plastic used to make film and records

coaxed (kohkst): influenced by gentle urging

commotion (kuh **moh** shuhn): noisy excitement and confusion

confines: boundary or limit

conifer (**kah** nuh fur): a tree or shrub that produces cones and has leaves that look like needles or scales

courtesy (**kur** tuh see): a polite or generous act

crevasse (kri **vas**): a crack in ice or rock

croup (kroop): a throat condition, usually occurring in children, that causes a barking cough

cultivate (**kuhl** tuh vayt): raise or assist the growth of crops by tilling or labor

curiosity (kyur ee **ah** suh tee): an eager desire to learn

cylindrical (suh **lin** dri kuhl): having a long round shape

deciduous (di **si** juh wuhs): having parts that fall off at the end of a period of growth

depression (di **presh** uhn): period of low activity in business

diaphragm: the muscle that allows lungs to inhale and exhale

donation: something given to help those in need

epidemic (ep uh **dem** ik): spreading widely and affecting many people at the same time

foe: enemy

freewheeling (free **whee** ling): not bound by formal rules or guidelines

hemisphere (**he** muh sfir): one of the halves of the sky, imagined as a giant dome, that can be seen from earth

heritage (**her** uh tij): the traditions, achievements, and beliefs that are part of the history of a group of people

hibernate (**hı** bur nayt): pass all or part of the winter in an inactive state in which body temperature drops and breathing slows

horizontal (hor uh **zahn** tuhl): lying flat or level

hyacinth (**hı** uh sinth): a plant with stalks of fragrant flowers shaped like bells

internationally (in tur **nash** uh nuh lee): active or known in many nations

irritation (ir uh **tay** shuhn): anger or annoyance

justice of the peace: someone who is elected or appointed to perform marriages and make decisions on minor court cases

kerosene (**ker** uh seen): a thin oil used as a fuel

kit (kit): a young, fur-bearing animal

knickers: loose-fitting pants that button just below the knee

legacy: something (like memories or knowledge) that comes from the past or a person of the past

linguistics (ling **gwis** tiks): the study of human speech and languages

literary critic: someone who studies, explains, and judges pieces of writing

lore (lor): common traditions or beliefs

merciful (**mur** si fuhl): having compassion or showing kind treatment

mischievous (**mis** chuh vuhs): showing a spirit of fun or playfulness

naturalist (**na** chuh ruh list): a person who studies plants and animals as they live in nature

naysayer (**nay** say ur): a person who says something will not work or is not possible

nocturnal (nok **tur** nuhl): active at night

nuisance (**noo** suhns): an annoying or troublesome person, thing, or situation

ornithologist (or nuh **thah** luh jist): a person who studies birds

pandemic (pan **de** mik): an occurrence in which a disease spreads very quickly and affects a large number of people over a wide area

paralyzed (**per** uh lızd): unable to move all or part of the body

pharmacy (**fahr** muh see): the science of preparing and providing medicine

pistil (**pis** tuhl): the part in the center of a flower that produces the seed

plummeted (**pluh** muh tid): fell straight down

pneumonia (nu **moh** nyuh): a serious illness affecting the lungs that is marked by fever, cough, and difficulty in breathing

post-graduate (pohst **gra** juh wuht): continuing formal education after graduating from college

presided: was in charge

prohibition (proh huh **bish** uhn): a law or order that stops something from being used or done

publisher (**pub** lish ur): a person or company that prepares printed works, like books, for sale

quarantined (**kwawr** uhn teend): separated from other people to prevent the spread of disease

rabies: a deadly disease of the nervous system that affects animals and can be passed on to people by the bite of an infected animal

seeped: flowed slowly through a small opening

stamen (**stay** muhn): the part of a flower that produces pollen

stylus (**stı** luhs): a very small, pointed piece of metal that touches a record and produces sound when the record is played

temptation (tem **tay** shuhn): strong desire

threshing: separating the seed from a harvested plant by beating

thunderous (**thun** duh ruhs): very loud

translated (**trans** lay tid): turned from one language into another

treacherous (**tre** chuh ruhs): not safe because of hidden dangers

verdict: a decision reached by a jury or judge

Reading Group Guide and Activities

Discussion Questions

❧ How was Sterling's childhood adventurous and unusual? Can you list at least 3 people, things, or ideas from his childhood that influenced his writing as an adult? What would you write about your own life so far? Have you had any adventures? Rascal helped Sterling feel less alone in difficult times. Can you describe how and why? What people, places, or things make you feel less lonely sometimes, too?

❧ Sterling's childhood was filled with many important changes in society, such as the invention of cars and airplanes. Think about society today. How has society continued to change since Sterling's time? Do you think Sterling would like these changes? Why or why not?

Activities:

❧ Sterling learned that wild animals need to live in the wild, not in his home. Imagine you could have any pet you wanted. Would it be real or imaginary? What would it look like? What would it eat? What would you call it? Draw your pet and write a short story about your life together.

❧ Sterling North loved his hometown of Edgerton. Make a list of the top 5 things you love about your own town or neighborhood. Then use that list to make an illustrated collage that showcases all of your favorite things about your town or neighborhood.

❧ Sterling's mother was one of his greatest influences. Create an award certificate for the person (or people) in your life who matter the most. Write a one-sentence summary of why they are so important to you. For example: "This award goes to my Grandma Millie for always smiling and laughing at my jokes." Be sure to draw a fancy border and illustrate your certificate. You could create it by hand or on the computer!

❧ For teachers: Create a classroom version of *Books on Trial*. Divide your class into 3 groups: Pro, Con, and Judges. Assign roles and responsibilities to each group (tell what you like about the book, what page it's on, why you like it; tell what you dislike about the book, what page it's on, why you dislike it; listen to both sides and decided if the book is Good or Bad; etc). Use a modified debate structure so that all students have a chance to voice their opinion. Remember to help your judges base their decisions on the arguments, not on whether they like the book themselves!

To Learn More about Sterling North's Work

Books

Abe Lincoln: Log Cabin to the White House, Houghton Mifflin Company, North Star series, 1963.

Captured by the Mohawks, Dell Publishing, 1967.

George Washington, Frontier Colonel, Sterling Publishing Company, 2006.

Little Rascal, E. P. Dutton and Co., 1965.

Midnight and Jeremiah, Winston, 1943.

Raccoons Are the Brightest People, Avon Books, 1968.

Rascal: A Memoir of a Better Era, Puffin Books, 1963.

Thoreau of Walden Pond, Houghton Mifflin Company, North Star series, 1959.

So Dear to My Heart, Doubleday, 1947.

The Wolfling: A Documentary Novel of the Eighteen-Seventies, Puffin Books, 1969.

Young Thomas Edison, Houghton Mifflin Company, North Star series, 1958.

Please note, some of the titles listed above have been republished by companies other than those listed.

Films

Rascal, Walt Disney Productions, 1969.

So Dear To My Heart, Walt Disney Productions, 1947.

Acknowledgments

It is with great gratitude that I was able to write this book with the help of people who knew Sterling North very well. His daughter Arielle North Olson and son David North were invaluable sources of information, graciously sharing their memories in words and photos, which helped bring their father to life.

Walt Diedrick, a lifetime resident of Edgerton, provided me with more valuable information about Sterling's life and time in Edgerton, through photos and actual visits to Sterling's many childhood haunts. Fortunately I was privy to one of Mr. Diedrick's regularly organized tours that included Sterling's favorite fishing hole, the church steeple where his pet crow Poe carried shining treasures, the barn wall where Sterling carved words that can still be seen and, of course, Sterling's boyhood home, which has been beautifully restored by several Edgerton residents under Mr. Diedrick's tutelage.

Members of the Sterling North Society graciously opened their doors and vast archives to me during the course of my research, providing me with access to valuable letters, posters, and artifacts that were an important part of Sterling's life.

All of these people helped supplement the many facets of Sterling North's life that I was able to glean from the written words he himself left behind.

After the gathering of information, and the placing of words on paper, no book is ever complete without the careful eye of an editor. I definitely had that in Carrie Kilman of the Wisconsin Historical Society Press. Ms. Kilman's sense of word structure and clarity helped make the pages of this book more accessible to the audience of young readers for which they are meant. I am most appreciative of her assistance.

And, of course, no book is ready for publication without attending to all the details of final production, such as layout and visual additions. My thanks to production editor Diane Drexler and all those who work with her at the Wisconsin Historical Society Press.

Index

This index points you to the pages where you can read about persons, places, and ideas. If you do not find the word you are looking for, try to think of another word that means about the same thing.

When you see a page number in **bold** it means there is a picture on that page.